Sight Word Readers
Handbook
A Guide to Using Content-Area Sight Word Readers

Table of Contents

Introduction

So that pre-emergent and emergent readers are better able to develop literacy skills, Newmark Learning created Sight Word Readers. While you read many rich texts to children at this age, you also need to give them leveled texts they can more easily absorb. The familiar Science, Math, and Social Studies themes explored in these books are supported by simple, repetitive sentence patterns, rebus pictures, and real-world photographs to help young readers build confidence.

Sight Word Readers is ideal for small-group instruction. The series is specifically designed so that pre-emergent and emergent readers have the opportunity to explore new facets of literacy well supported by the teacher.

Through Sight Word Readers, students will:

- Learn to make predictions with picture support
- Develop oral language structures
- Develop visual perception skills
- Become familiar with print
- Develop early reading strategies
- Boost letter recognition and acquire beginning phonetic elements
- Achieve automaticity with a beginning sight word vocabulary, based on the Marie Clay High-Frequency Word List and the Dolch Pre-Primer Sight Vocabulary
- Become motivated to read and reread
- Build knowledge of everyday Math, Science, and Social Studies themes
- Increase concept word vocabulary
- Build oral reading fluency
- Develop silent reading and tracking skills
- Reflect on texts
- Use their imagination
- Improve listening skills
- Extend attention span
- Develop confidence
- Develop interpersonal, social, and collaborative skills
- Have fun while engaged in purposeful reading practice

Why Teach Sight Words?

Beginning readers are confronted with the formidable task of trying to decode words while also trying to understand the text. The combined attention demands of decoding and comprehension are often greater than what the beginning reader can handle (Samuels, Schermer, and Reinking, 1992). This makes reading a slow and laborious task for many students. Comprehension often suffers because the beginning reader can handle only one task at a time: decoding or comprehension. The goal is to help readers develop automaticity so they can devote more attention to comprehension.

One way students can develop fluency is by instantly recognizing words that are used with high frequency in beginning reading texts. There are 100 words that account for approximately 50 percent of the words used in print (Fry, Fountoukidis, and Polk, 1985; Adams, 1990). Interestingly, the words **a**, **and**, **for**, **he**, **is**, **in**, **it**, **of**, **that**, **the**, **to**, **was**, and **you** account for 25 percent of the words in print (Johns, 1980). Therefore, by teaching students to recognize these commonly used words, we can make the process of reading much more fluent and automatic for them. Knowledge of high-frequency words is necessary for fluent reading. The Sight Word Readers series exposes young readers to forty-nine high-frequency words.

Words such as **in** and **it** are considered to be regular because they follow regular sound/symbol patterns and can be decoded. Many high-frequency words, however, are irregular because they do not follow regular sound/symbol relationships. These words cannot be sounded out and need to be memorized. Many of the words can be easily confused by students: for example, **of** and **for**; **their**, **them**, **then**; **were**, **where**, **what**, etc. Students do not learn these irregular words as quickly and easily as they learn regular words. They need to be taught these words with explicit instruction (Blevins, 1998).

Building Literacy Skills

With Sight Word Readers your students will:

- Practice utilizing print features
- Make predictions and draw upon prior knowledge
- Listen to models of fluent reading
- Echo-read with the support of their teacher and peers
- Make connections to familiar people, places, and events
- Learn new sight words

In *Literacy Lessons Designed for Individuals (Part One)*, Marie Clay says, "Observation involves more than hearing children read every day. It involves being a teacher who interacts with the child, who notices the child's responses to the story, its language and its meanings, and who takes the time to gather evidence of how the child is working on print. The teacher must be reflective and responsive to the negotiations of the child." Following are some of the specific skills you can teach, or observe, as students engage in echo-reading, choral-reading, and independent practice of Sight Word Readers.

Emergent Reading Strategies

- Makes predictions about the text
- Reads fluently
- Problem solves on one or two things
- Knows a small core of sight words
- Stops when reading does not make sense and searches the picture as well as the print
- Rereads by returning to the beginning of the sentence
- Cross-checks prediction at point of difficulty with the picture and print
- Rereads at point of difficulty and articulates the first letter of the problem word
- Discusses and/or retells the story

Concepts About Print

- Can point to the cover
- Can point to the title
- Can point to the author's name
- Knows how to open the book
- Can point to the first page
- Can point to the top and bottom of the page
- Knows which parts of the page are words and which parts are pictures
- Knows where to start reading
- Knows which way to move his or her finger while reading
- Can point to each word while reading a line
- Can count the number of words in the line
- Knows where to start reading next
- Can point to an uppercase letter
- Can point to the first letter in a word
- Can point to the last letter in a word
- Can point to, name, and tell the purpose of a period
- Can point to, name, and tell the purpose of a question mark
- Can point to, name, and tell the purpose of an exclamation point
- Can point to, name, and tell the purpose of a comma

Fluency Skills

- Reads smoothly with minimal breaks
- Reads with appropriate pauses
- Stops at the end of each sentence
- Reads question marks
- Reads exclamation marks
- Reads commas

Sight Words

a	all	am	and	are	at	be	big	can	dad
do	down	eat	get	go	goes	had	has	have	he
here	I	in	is	it	like	little	look	me	mom
my	play	said	see	she	some	that	the	there	they
this	to	up	wants	we	went	will	with	you	

Content Words

See the Correlation Chart on pages 18–21 for the specific Science, Social Studies, or Math vocabulary in each title.

Using the Books

Each book in the Sight Word Readers series adheres to a strict structure and has one repetitive sentence frame that supports both pre-emergent and emergent readers. Repeated reading of the same sentence pattern helps students develop confidence and mastery of a few sight words, and the short sentences (usually five or fewer words) with no return sweep help students track the text. To support English-language development, sentence patterns reflect natural, spoken language, and question marks and exclamation points provide opportunities to model-read with appropriate expression.

Texts provide opportunities for repeated readings.

Inside Front Cover

Shows the supported state curriculum standard.

Lists sight word vocabulary and content vocabulary.

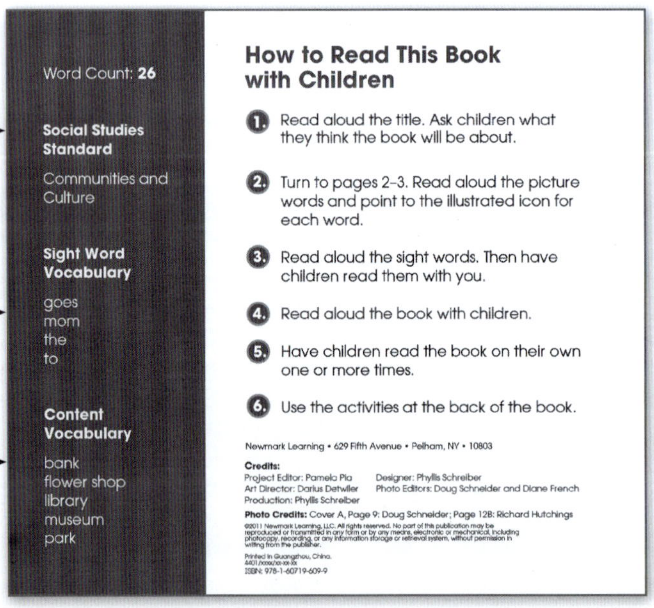

Word Count: **26**

Social Studies Standard

Communities and Culture

Sight Word Vocabulary

goes
mom
the
to

Content Vocabulary

bank
flower shop
library
museum
park

How to Read This Book with Children

1. Read aloud the title. Ask children what they think the book will be about.
2. Turn to pages 2–3. Read aloud the picture words and point to the illustrated icon for each word.
3. Read aloud the sight words. Then have children read them with you.
4. Read aloud the book with children.
5. Have children read the book on their own one or more times.
6. Use the activities at the back of the book.

Newmark Learning • 629 Fifth Avenue • Pelham, NY • 10803

Credits:
Project Editor: Pamela Pia
Designer: Phyllis Schreiber
Art Director: Darius Detwiler
Photo Editors: Doug Schneider and Diane French
Production: Phyllis Schreiber

Photo Credits: Cover A, Page 9: Doug Schneider; Page 12B: Richard Hutchings

Printed in Guangzhou, China.
4401/xxxx/xx-xx-xx
ISBN: 978-1-60719-609-9

Picture Words

(pages 2–3)

Every book has a spread that precedes the actual text so teachers can front-load, or introduce, needed words.

Picture words are key content words that are supported visually in the text with photographs and rebuses.

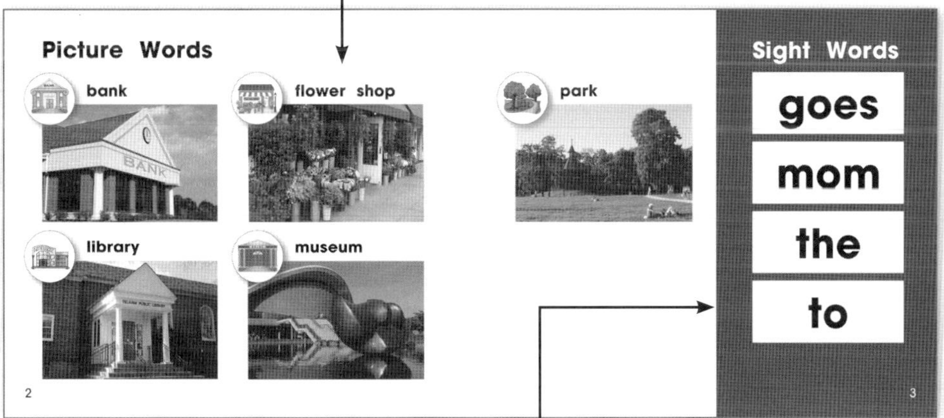

Sight words are based on the Marie Clay and Dolch lists of words commonly learned at the pre-emergent and emergent levels. A total of forty-nine sight words are used throughout the series. Many words appear in multiple titles.

Text

(pages 4–12)

Rebuses provide the highest level of picture support for young readers who cannot yet decode text.

Full-color photographs convey the text's context and provide additional direct picture support. The photographs also stimulate rich oral language and reinforce the key concepts.

Beginning readers learn to recognize basic forms of punctuation (period, question mark, exclamation point).

Inside Back Cover

A graphic organizer on the inside back cover provides a review of sight words plus opportunities for summarizing and retelling.

Activities for Differentiated Literacy Instruction

Use the reproducible letter cards, sight word cards, and sentence patterns found in this handbook, along with your own readily available classroom materials, to differentiate literacy instruction for pre-emergent and emergent readers. See the chart on page 10 for additional activities to use in small groups or literacy centers.

Letter Cards

The letter cards on pages 47–53 include one of each uppercase letter and two of each lowercase letter. Students can use the letter cards to:

- Visually match letters to the text
- Make sight words

Sight Word Cards

The Sight Word Readers sight word cards, based on the Marie Clay High-Frequency Word List and the Dolch Pre-Primer Sight Vocabulary, are on pages 54–59. To introduce each word:

- Say the word aloud and run your finger under it as you say it.
- Ask students to say the word with you.
- Ask students to spell the word aloud as you point to each letter.
- Invite students to write the word in the air as you point to each letter.
- Help students locate the word in the script.

Sentence Patterns

The sentence patterns, found on pages 22–46, are specific to each book. Students can write or draw to complete the sentences or cut the sentence patterns apart and:

- Match the words to the text
- Scramble and rearrange the sentences
- Make up new oral sentences using the patterns

Activities for Differentiated Literacy Instruction		
Activity	**Pre-Emergent Readers**	**Emergent Readers**
Use the reproducible letter cards.	• Match letters with like characteristics—tall letters such as **f** and **t**, short letters such as **o** and **m**, letters with all straight lines such as **l** and **x**, and letters with all curved lines such as **c** and **s**. • Match uppercase to lowercase letters. • Using several sets, sort visually similar letters such as **b** and **d** or **p** and **q**.	• Name an item in a picture and locate the letter card that has the same initial sound. • Spell out a sentence in the book, and then read it to a partner.
Use the reproducible sight word cards and sentence patterns.	• Visually match the sight words to the words in the sentence patterns. • Using two sets of sight word cards or sentence patterns, play the game *Memory* by turning them facedown on the table and trying to turn up two that match.	• Practice reading the sight words and sentence patterns with a partner. • Use the sight words to create new sentence patterns. • Locate the sight words and sentence patterns in other emergent reading materials.
Make theme books.	• Make a group rebus book based on the theme and one sentence pattern from the script. • Example: For *We Like Vegetables*, ask students to cut out pictures of vegetables from grocery ads or magazines. • Write "I like" on each page, followed by one of the photos and a period. • Write the name of the vegetable under the photo on each page. • Read the book together and add it to the reading corner.	• Make individual books based on the theme and one sentence pattern from the script. • Example: For *We Like Vegetables*, ask students to cut out pictures of vegetables from grocery ads or magazines. • Ask students to write "I like" on each page, followed by one of the photos and a period. • Write the name of the vegetable under the photo on each page. • Invite students to read their books to a partner and add them to their personal book boxes.

Assessment

Sight Word Readers provides two different tools for assessment. Instructions for implementing each assessment follow.

Concepts About Print Assessment

Make a copy of page 60 to record data for each student. One by one, hand students a book and ask them to locate or demonstrate the targeted text feature or skill. Record the results on the data sheets, and use the results to pull together small groups of students for reteaching. Re-administer the assessment periodically to document students' growth in concepts about print.

Sight Word Assessment

Make copies of pages 61–62 to record data for each student. Write the sight words for your targeted script on the board. Alternatively, display the appropriate sight word cards from pages 54–59 of this handbook. One by one, ask students to read the words to you. Record the results on the student data sheets, and use the results to pull together small groups of students for reteaching.

Sight Word Lesson

Introduce the Sight Words

Tell students that in order to become good readers, they need to memorize certain words. Explain that by doing so, they will read faster—they will no longer need to spend time working out the words. Emphasize that students will need to practice reading the words over and over again in order to memorize them.

Follow these steps to introduce each sight word in the lesson.

- Write the first high-frequency word on the board and explain that it is one of the words students will memorize.
- Say the word and run your finger under it as you say it. Then have students say the word with you.
- Point to different students and ask them to read the word.
- Hold up the corresponding word card and have students read it.
- Have students spell the word aloud as you point to each letter.
- Have them write the word in the air as you point to each letter.

Practice the Sight Words

Use the word cards for practice. Quickly show students the word cards, one at a time, and have them say the words. Mix up the cards each time. Then have volunteers take a card and match it to the appropriate word on the board.

Review Previously Taught Sight Words

Use the word cards for a quick review of previously taught high-frequency words that appear in the Sight Word Readers book.

- Hold up a card and ask what the word is. If students have trouble remembering the word, quickly tell them the word, then ask them to repeat it.
- Ask several students to say the word.
- Mix that word card with the other word cards you are using in the lesson, and move on to the next word card.
- Include the new sight words in the practice. If students forget a new word, tell them what it is, then ask them to repeat it.
- Use the new sight word cards and the review sight word cards to create a sentence pattern from the book in a pocket chart or along the ledge of the board.
- Provide a model for students by saying a sentence using the sight words and adding a new content word. Point to each sight word as you say it.
- Ask individual students to create oral sentences by using the sentence pattern provided and adding a new content word.
- Select two students. Have one student point to each sight word while the other says a new sentence.

Teacher Tip

The practice should be fast-paced, explicit, and repeated.

Apply the Sight Words Using the Sight Word Readers Book

BOOK INTRODUCTION Students are now ready to read the words in connected text. Begin the introduction by giving a brief summary of the text. Draw students' attention to the front cover of the book and read the title and the name of the author(s). Encourage students to discuss the photograph on the cover of the book. Allow time for students to discuss what they know about the topic.

FIRST READING Read the book aloud at a fluent and expressive pace. At the same time, point underneath each word with a pointer. Precise pointing allows you to model directionality and one-to-one matching as students attend to the print. Then ask students to join in reading as you read the book again. Have students point to each word as a page is read.

USING THE WORD CARDS

- Ask volunteers to take a word card from the stack and match it to a word in the book. They should say the word aloud as they match the card to the word.
- Have students use the word cards to create sentences in the pocket chart. They can duplicate sentences in the book or create their own. Have students read their sentences.
- Ask individual students to read words in the sentence as you point to the words.
- Have volunteers read individual words in the text. Remind them that their finger should be pointing under the exact word they are reading.

Spell the Sight Words Using the Letter Cards

Use the blackline masters to duplicate the letters you need for the lesson.

- Write the sight word on the board.
- Distribute the appropriate letter cards to each student.
- Ask students to construct the word three times using the model on the board. Ask students to say the word slowly as they construct it. Scaffold the task as needed. Remind students to think about how the word looks.
- Erase the visual model on the board. Instruct students to construct the word three times without the model. Make sure they say the word slowly as they construct it. Have students check their word by running their finger under the word and saying it slowly. Ask them to think about how the word looks.
- Prompt students to write the word on their dry-erase board several times. Make sure they say the word aloud as they write it. Instruct them to erase the word and write it again quickly for fluency.

Teacher Tip

Laminate the letter cards for future use. Make multiple copies so that each student has a set to work with.

Read Independently

Provide opportunities for repeated reading of the book both independently and with a partner. Observe students as they are reading. The behaviors identified below can help you evaluate students' processing behaviors on text reading.

- Reads fluently
- Has one-to-one matching
- Knows directionality
- Reads high-frequency words fluently
- Self-monitors as he or she reads

Write

Innovate on the Text

Show students how they can write their own story using a simple pattern from the Sight Word Readers book.

- Give each student a reproducible writing page. Reread some of the sentences in the book to remind students of the pattern.
- Read aloud the model sentence on the reproducible page, asking individual students to supply a word that would make sense.
- Tell students they are going to write a sentence similar to those in the book one or more times. Instruct them to look at the sentence on the reproducible page and read it aloud. Then tell them to cover the model sentence with their hand or a piece of paper. Have them write the sentence from memory, saying each word softly and listening to the sounds as they write. Tell them to complete the sentence by drawing a picture of something that makes sense.

- When students have finished writing their sentence(s), have them check their work by comparing their sentence(s) with the model sentence at the top of the page. Encourage students to write the sentence several more times on the back of the reproducible page for additional practice.
- Students' pages can be compiled into a class book that can be placed in the classroom library and used for further sight word practice during independent reading.

Learning Center Activities

Use some or all of the following activities to provide independent practice.

Word Cards

CONCENTRATION GAME Provide two copies of each word in an envelope. Have students spread all the cards facedown on the table. Instruct them to take turns turning over two cards. If the two cards they turn over show the same word, they get to keep the pair.

BOARD GAME 1 Use a game board from a commercial game or make up your own. Have students turn the stack of word cards facedown. Instruct them to take turns drawing a card. Tell them that if they can read the word on the card, they get to move two spaces on the board. If they can use the word correctly in a sentence, they get to move four spaces. Have them place the used card on the bottom of the stack. Then the next student takes a turn.

BOARD GAME 2 Create a game board on which a sight word is written in each space. Tell students to throw the dice and move the number of spaces indicated. As they move they must read each sight word along the way. If they make a mistake, they must return to the space they occupied before rolling the dice.

WORD RACE Have students take turns turning over a word card from a stack of sight word cards. The first player to say the word correctly gets to keep the card.

WORD MATCH Have students match the words on the cards to words in books and/ or magazines provided. This can be turned into a game by having students race to see who can find a word first.

PICK AND SAY Have students take turns drawing a word card from a stack of high-frequency word cards. They must say the word and use it in a sentence. If they are correct, they keep the card.

Teacher Tip

Duplicated copies of the word and letter cards can be laminated and put in envelopes for students to use at a learning center.

Letter Cards

SPELLING Have students use the letters in the envelope to spell words and record them in a journal or on paper.

LETTER DRAW Have students draw letter cards from a stack. Tell them that when they think they have enough letters, they should spell a word. If they spell the word correctly, they get points.

LETTER MATCH Have students draw a word card and then find the letters used to spell the word.

BOARD GAME Use the game board created for Board Game 2. Have students roll the dice and move along the board the indicated number of spaces. Tell them they must use letter cards to spell the word written in the space on which they land. If they cannot spell the word, they must go back to where they were before they rolled the dice.

The Lesson Sequence

INTRODUCE
the new sight words using the explicit steps provided.

PRACTICE
the new sight words using the word cards.

big

can

All sight words in the program are provided in this guide in the form of reproducible pages.

REVIEW
previously taught sight words that appear in the book using the word cards.

go

They

APPLY
the sight words in connected text by having students read the book with you.

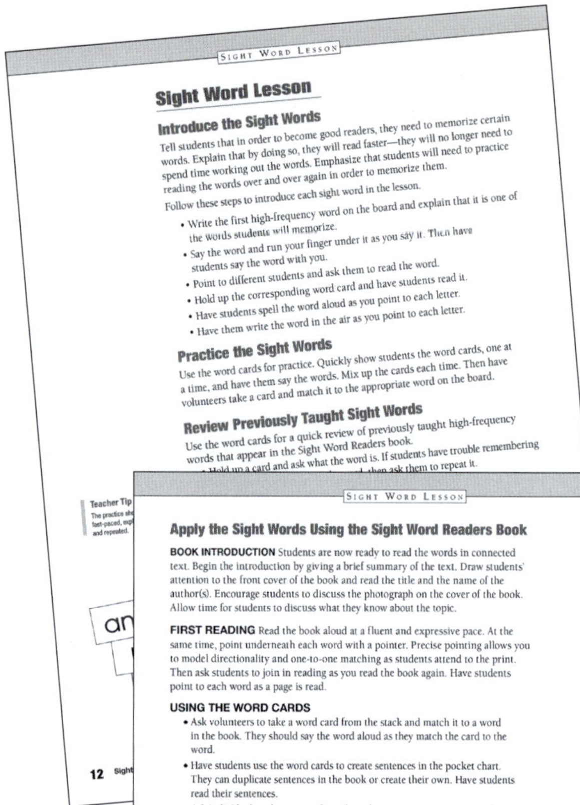

Sight Word Lesson

Introduce the Sight Words

Tell students that in order to become good readers, they need to memorize certain words. Explain that by doing so, they will read faster—they will no longer need to spend time working out the words. Emphasize that students will need to practice reading the words over and over again in order to memorize them.

Follow these steps to introduce each sight word in the lesson.

- Write the first high-frequency word on the board and explain that it is one of the words students will memorize.
- Say the word and run your finger under it as you say it. Then have students say the word with you.
- Point to different students and ask them to read the word.
- Hold up the corresponding word card and have students read it.
- Have students spell the word aloud as you point to each letter.
- Have them write the word in the air as you point to each letter.

Practice the Sight Words

Use the word cards for practice. Quickly show students the word cards, one at a time, and have them say the words. Mix up the cards each time. Then have volunteers take a card and match it to the appropriate word on the board.

Review Previously Taught Sight Words

Use the word cards for a quick review of previously taught high-frequency words that appear in the Sight Word Readers book. If students have trouble remembering

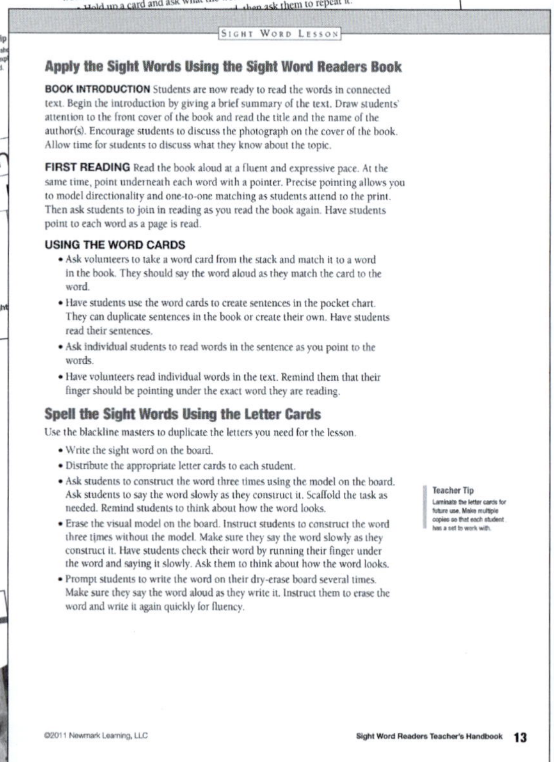

Apply the Sight Words Using the Sight Word Readers Book

BOOK INTRODUCTION Students are now ready to read the words in connected text. Begin the introduction by giving a brief summary of the text. Draw students' attention to the front cover of the book and read the title and the name of the author(s). Encourage students to discuss the photograph on the cover of the book. Allow time for students to discuss what they know about the topic.

FIRST READING Read the book aloud at a fluent and expressive pace. At the same time, point underneath each word with a pointer. Precise pointing allows you to model directionality and one-to-one matching as students attend to the print. Then ask students to join in reading as you read the book again. Have students point to each word as a page is read.

USING THE WORD CARDS

- Ask volunteers to take a word card from the stack and match it to a word in the book. They should say the word aloud as they match the card to the word.
- Have students use the word cards to create sentences in the pocket chart. They can duplicate sentences in the book or create their own. Have students read their sentences.
- Ask individual students to read words in the sentence as you point to the words.
- Have volunteers read individual words in the text. Remind them that their finger should be pointing under the exact word they are reading.

Spell the Sight Words Using the Letter Cards

Use the blackline masters to duplicate the letters you need for the lesson.

- Write the sight word on the board.
- Distribute the appropriate letter cards to each student.
- Ask students to construct the word three times using the model on the board. Ask students to say the word slowly as they construct it. Scaffold the task as needed. Remind students to think about how the word looks.
- Erase the visual model on the board. Instruct students to construct the word three times without the model. Make sure they say the word slowly as they construct it. Have students check their word by running their finger under the word and saying it slowly. Ask them to think about how the word looks.
- Prompt students to write the word on their dry-erase board several times. Make sure they say the word aloud as they write it. Instruct them to erase the word and write it again quickly for fluency.

Teacher Tip
Laminate the letter cards for future use. Make multiple copies so that each student has a set to work with.

get

Sight words are repeated many times in each of the 48 books. The use of rebuses makes sentences meaningful.

Use word cards to duplicate sentences in the book and for one-to-one matching.

Direct and Explicit Instruction in High-Frequency Words

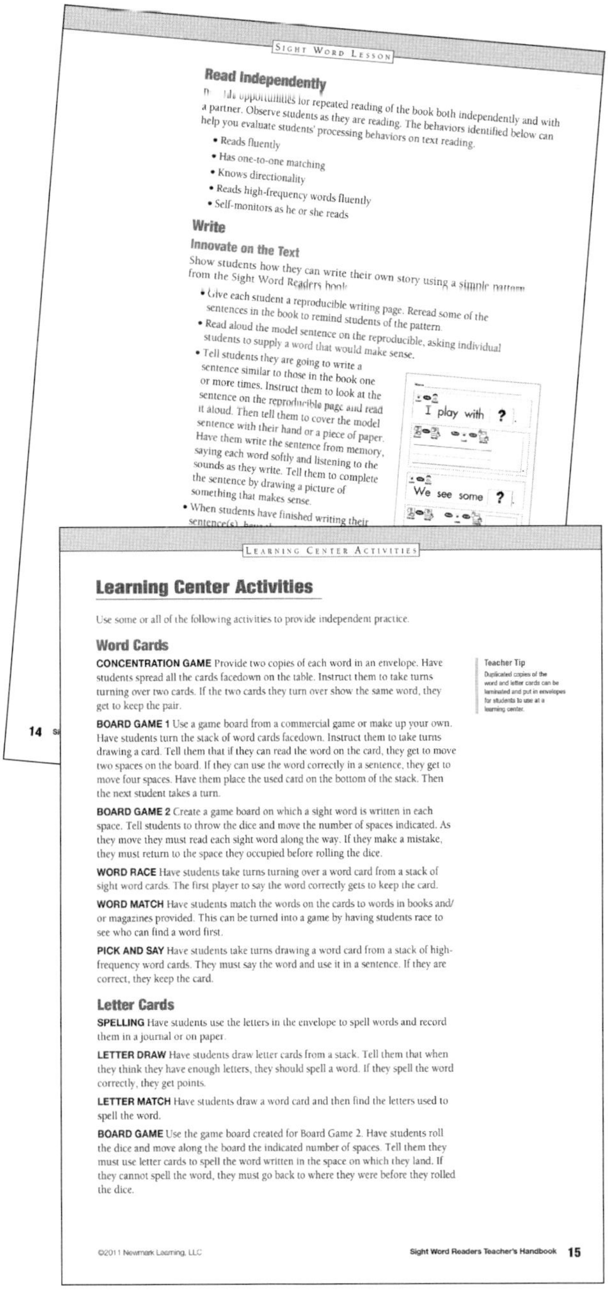
Sight Word Lesson

Read Independently

P[illegible] opportunities for repeated reading of the book both independently and with a partner. Observe students as they are reading. The behaviors identified below can help you evaluate students' processing behaviors on text reading.

- Reads fluently
- Has one-to-one matching
- Knows directionality
- Reads high-frequency words fluently
- Self-monitors as he or she reads

Write

Innovate on the Text

Show students how they can write their own story using a simple pattern from the Sight Word Readers book.

- Give each student a reproducible writing page. Reread some of the sentences in the book to remind students of the pattern.
- Read aloud the model sentence on the reproducible, asking individual students to supply a word that would make sense.
- Tell students they are going to write a sentence similar to those in the book one or more times. Instruct them to look at the sentence on the reproducible page and read it aloud. Then tell them to cover the model sentence with their hand or a piece of paper. Have them write the sentence from memory, saying each word softly and listening to the sounds as they write. Tell them to complete the sentence by drawing a picture of something that makes sense.
- When students have finished writing their sentence(s), [illegible]

I play with ?.

We see some ?.

14

Learning Center Activities

Learning Center Activities

Use some or all of the following activities to provide independent practice.

Word Cards

CONCENTRATION GAME Provide two copies of each word in an envelope. Have students spread all the cards facedown on the table. Instruct them to take turns turning over two cards. If the two cards they turn over show the same word, they get to keep the pair.

BOARD GAME 1 Use a game board from a commercial game or make up your own. Have students turn the stack of word cards facedown. Instruct them to take turns drawing a card. Tell them that if they can read the word on the card, they get to move two spaces on the board. If they can use the word correctly in a sentence, they get to move four spaces. Have them place the used card on the bottom of the stack. Then the next student takes a turn.

BOARD GAME 2 Create a game board on which a sight word is written in each space. Tell students to throw the dice and move the number of spaces indicated. As they move they must read each sight word along the way. If they make a mistake, they must return to the space they occupied before rolling the dice.

WORD RACE Have students take turns turning over a word card from a stack of sight word cards. The first player to say the word correctly gets to keep the card.

WORD MATCH Have students match the words on the cards to words in books and/or magazines provided. This can be turned into a game by having students race to see who can find a word first.

PICK AND SAY Have students take turns drawing a word card from a stack of high-frequency word cards. They must say the word and use it in a sentence. If they are correct, they keep the card.

Teacher Tip
Duplicated copies of the word and letter cards can be laminated and put in envelopes for students to use at a learning center.

Letter Cards

SPELLING Have students use the letters in the envelope to spell words and record them in a journal or on paper.

LETTER DRAW Have students draw letter cards from a stack. Tell them that when they think they have enough letters, they should spell a word. If they spell the word correctly, they get points.

LETTER MATCH Have students draw a word card and then find the letters used to spell the word.

BOARD GAME Use the game board created for Board Game 2. Have students roll the dice and move along the board the indicated number of spaces. Tell them they must use letter cards to spell the word written in the space on which they land. If they cannot spell the word, they must go back to where they were before they rolled the dice.

©2011 Newmark Learning, LLC — Sight Word Readers Teacher's Handbook 15

Learning Center ACTIVITIES

PRACTICE INDEPENDENTLY

Use learning center activities for practice.

Use the letter and word cards to create learning center practice activities. Ideas are included in the model lesson on pages 12–14.

WRITE

Have students write sentences using the sentence pattern in the book.

Each title has a corresponding tracing and writing reproducible.

READ INDEPENDENTLY

Provide repeated reading practice with the 48 Sight Word Readers.

Have students use Sight Word Readers in independent activities.

SPELL

Have students spell each new word using the letter cards.

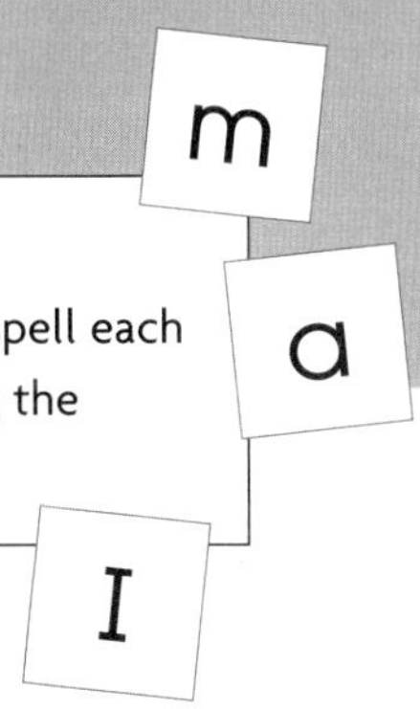

Reproducible pages of letter cards are provided in this guide.

Sight Word Readers Correlation Chart

Title	Subject	Sight Words
Animal Babies	Math	I, play, with
Animals on the Farm	Science	see, some, we
At Grandma's House	Social Studies	had, we
At My School	Social Studies	a, is, mom
At the Shore	Science	at, look, the, we
Big Pet, Little Pet	Math	big, is, little, this
Count Around the Room	Math	has, he
Count at the Baseball Field	Math	have, we
Count on Me	Math	has, she
Counting With Mom	Math	and, I, mom, see
Dad Likes New Clothes	Social Studies	a, dad, wants
Finding Shapes With Dad	Math	dad, said, see, the
Finding Stripes	Math	see, the, with
Going Up and Down	Science	down, go, the, they, up
I Am Active	Science	am, I
I Go!	Science	a, go, I, in
I Like the Spring!	Science	I, like, the
I Like to Play Sports	Social Studies	I, like, play, to
In Our Town	Social Studies	goes, mom, the, to
In the Band	Social Studies	at, look, the
In the Water	Science	I, in, play, the
Jobs Around Town	Social Studies	are, we
Look and See	Science	at, look, that
Look at the Coins	Math	a, here, is

Content Vocabulary	Sentence Pattern
bunnies, chick, kittens, lambs, puppies	I play with ________.
chickens, cows, horses, pigs, sheep	We see some ________.
cheese, fruit, milk, pizza, popcorn	We had ________.
bus driver, coach, janitor, nurse, teacher	Mom is a ________.
clam, crab, snail, starfish, whale	We look at the ________.
bird, cat, dog, horse, rabbit	This ________ is big/little.
bed, chairs, hats, room, shells	He has ________.
baseballs, bats, caps, field, gloves	We have ________.
feet, fingers, hands, nose, toes	She has ________.
ants, beetles, butterfly, grasshoppers, spiders	Mom and I see ________.
coat, hat, shirt, sweater, vest	Dad wants a ________.
circle, rectangle, shapes, square, triangle	Dad said, "See the ________."
balls, chairs, sails, sandals, umbrellas	See the ______ with ______.
hill, ramp, rope, slide, steps	They go up/down the ______.
catching, jumping, kicking, running, swimming	I am ________.
bus, car, truck, van	I go in a ________.
bushes, eggs, flowers, leaves, spring	I like the ________.
basketball, football, soccer, tennis	I like to play ________.
bank, flower shop, library, museum, park	Mom goes to the ________.
band, drums, guitar, piano, trumpet	Look at the ________.
fountain, lake, pool, river, water	I play in the ________.
chefs, doctors, firefighters, police officers, teachers	We are ________.
desert, forest, mountain, river, waterfall	Look at that ________!
dime, dollar, nickel, penny, quarter	Here is a ________.

Sight Word Readers Correlation Chart

Title	Subject	Sight Words
Look at the Shapes	Math	can, see, the, you
Look at the Sky	Science	can, see, the, you
Look at the Weather	Science	I, can, see, the
My Family	Social Studies	is, me, my, this
My Favorite Places	Social Studies	I, the, to, went
My Home	Social Studies	at, look, my
My Pet	Social Studies	likes, me, my
My Town	Social Studies	here, is, my
On My Desk	Math	are, the, there
Our Tag Sale	Math	a, get, we
Playtime at Home	Math	play, they, with
See the Birds	Science	do, see, the, you
Snack Time	Science	had, some, they
They Grow Plants	Science	have, they, will
Time to Eat!	Math	at, eat, the
We Go to School	Social Studies	go, the, to, we
We Have Fruit	Science	have, we
We Like Birthdays	Social Studies	like, the, we
We Like Vegetables	Science	all, like, we
What Goes Up?	Science	goes, that, up
What Has Stripes?	Math	has, the
What Is the Time?	Math	is, it
When I Grow Up	Social Studies	a, be, I, will
With My Friends	Social Studies	a, all, to, we, went

Content Vocabulary	Sentence Pattern
circle, rectangle, shapes, square, triangle	Can you see the ________?
clouds, moon, sky, stars, sun	You can see the ________.
lightning, rain, snow, sun, wind	I can see the ________.
brother, dad, family, mom	This is ________.
aquarium, beach, lake, playground, pool	I went to the ________.
apartment, house, houseboat, igloo, tent	Look at my ________.
bird, cat, dog, fish, horse	My ________ likes me.
house, playground, school, street, town	Here is my ________.
crayons, erasers, markers, pencils, pens	The ________ are there.
dime, dollar, nickel, penny, quarter	We get a ________.
basketball, boats, cars, dolls, planes	They play with ________.
duck, eagle, owl, pelican, swan	Do you see the ________?
celery, cheese, crackers, pretzels, raisins	They had some ________.
corn, peppers, pumpkins, tomatoes, watermelon	They will have ________.
children, elephants, monkeys, polar bears, zebras	The ________ eat at ______.
cafeteria, classroom, gym, library, playground	We go to the ________.
apples, cherries, fruit, pears, watermelons	We have ________.
birthday party, cake, gifts, hats, pizza	We like the ________.
beans, carrots, cucumbers, peppers, vegetables	We all like ________.
ball, balloon, kite, plane, rocket	That ________ goes up.
caterpillar, fish, snake, stripes, tiger, zebra	The ________ has ________.
four o'clock, eight o'clock, nine o'clock, ten o'clock, two o'clock	It is ________.
doctor, farmer, firefighter, pilot, teacher	I will be a ________.
ball game, cookout, mall, park, restaurant	We all went to a ________.

Name ______________________________

Look and Read

I play with ? .

Cover and Write Then Look and Check

______________________________ .

Look and Read

We see some ? .

Cover and Write Then Look and Check

______________________________ .

Name ______________________________

Look and Read

We had ? .

Cover and Write Then Look and Check

______________________________ .

Look and Read

Mom is a ? .

Cover and Write Then Look and Check

______________________________ .

Name ______________________________

Look and Read

We look at the ?.

Cover and Write Then Look and Check

______________________________ .

Look and Read

This ? is big.

Cover and Write Then Look and Check

______________________________ .

Name ______________________________

Look and Read

This ? is little.

Cover and Write Then Look and Check

______________________________ .

Look and Read

He has ? .

Cover and Write Then Look and Check

______________________________ .

Name ____________________

Look **and** Read

We have ? .

Cover **and** Write **Then** Look **and** Check

________________________ .

Look **and** Read

She has ? .

Cover **and** Write **Then** Look **and** Check

________________________ .

Name ______________________________

Look and Read

Mom and I see ?.

Cover and Write Then Look and Check

______________________________ .

Look and Read

Dad wants a ?.

Cover and Write Then Look and Check

______________________________ .

Name ______________________________

Look and Read

Dad said, "See the ?."

Cover and Write Then Look and Check

______________________________ .

Look and Read

See the ? with ?.

Cover and Write Then Look and Check

______________________________ .

Name ______________________________

Look and Read

They go up the ? .

Cover and Write Then Look and Check

______________________________ .

Look and Read

They go down the ? .

Cover and Write Then Look and Check

______________________________ .

Name ______________________________

Look and Read

I am ? .

Cover and Write Then Look and Check

______________________________ .

Look and Read

I go in a ? .

Cover and Write Then Look and Check

______________________________ .

Name ____________________

Look and Read

I like the ?.

Cover and Write Then Look and Check

______________________________ .

Look and Read

I like to play ?.

Cover and Write Then Look and Check

______________________________ .

Name ____________________

Look and Read

Mom goes to the ? .

Cover and Write Then Look and Check

______________________________ .

Look and Read

Look at the ? .

Cover and Write Then Look and Check

______________________________ .

Name ______________________________

Look and Read

I play in the ? .

Cover and Write Then Look and Check

______________________________ .

Look and Read

We are ? .

Cover and Write Then Look and Check

______________________________ .

Name ______________________________

Look and Read

Look at that ? !

Cover and Write Then Look and Check

______________________________ .

Look and Read

Here is a ? .

Cover and Write Then Look and Check

______________________________ .

Name ______________________________

Look and Read

Can you see the ? ?

Cover and Write Then Look and Check

______________________________ .

Look and Read

You can see the ? .

Cover and Write Then Look and Check

______________________________ .

Name ________________________________

Look and Read

I can see the ? .

Cover and Write Then Look and Check

________________________________ .

Look and Read

This is ? .

Cover and Write Then Look and Check

________________________________ .

Name ______________________________

Look and Read

I went to the ?.

Cover and Write Then Look and Check

______________________________.

Look and Read

Look at my ?.

Cover and Write Then Look and Check

______________________________.

Name ______________________________

Look and Read

My ? likes me.

Cover and Write Then Look and Check

______________________ .

Look and Read

Here is my ? .

Cover and Write Then Look and Check

______________________ .

Name ____________________

Look and Read

The ? are there.

Cover and Write Then Look and Check

____________________ .

Look and Read

We get a ? .

Cover and Write Then Look and Check

____________________ .

Name ______________________________

Look and Read

They play with ? .

Cover and Write Then Look and Check

______________________________ .

Look and Read

Do you see the ? ?

Cover and Write Then Look and Check

______________________________ .

Name ______________________________

Look and Read

They had some ? .

Cover and Write Then Look and Check

______________________________ .

Look and Read

They will have ? .

Cover and Write Then Look and Check

______________________________ .

Name ______________________________

Look and Read

The ? eat at ? .

Cover and Write Then Look and Check

.

Look and Read

We go to the ? .

Cover and Write Then Look and Check

.

Name ________________________________

Look and Read

We have ? .

Cover and Write Then Look and Check

.

Look and Read

We like the ? .

Cover and Write Then Look and Check

.

Name ______________________________

Look and Read

We all like ? .

Cover and Write Then Look and Check

______________________________ .

Look and Read

That ? goes up.

Cover and Write Then Look and Check

______________________________ .

Name ______________________________

Look and Read

The ? has ? .

Cover and Write Then Look and Check

__________________________ .

Look and Read

It is ? .

Cover and Write Then Look and Check

__________________________ .

Name ______________________________

Look and Read

I will be a ?.

Cover and Write Then Look and Check

______________________________ .

Look and Read

We all went to a ?.

Cover and Write Then Look and Check

______________________________ .

A a a

B b b

C c c

D d d

E e e

F f f

G g g

H h h

I	i	i
J	j	j
K	k	k
L	l	l

M	m	m
N	n	n
O	o	o
P	p	p

Q	q	q
R	r	r
S	s	s
T	t	t

U	u	u
V	v	v
W	w	w
X	x	x

Y	y	y
Z	z	z
A	a	a
I	i	i

a

all

am

and

are

at

be

big

can

Can

Dad

do

Do

down

eat

get

go

goes

had

has

have

He

Here

here

I

in

is

It

like

likes

little

look

Look

me

Mom

my

My

play

said

see

See

she

She

some

that

That

the

The

there

They

This	to
up	wants
We	went
will	with
you	You

Concepts About Print Assessment

Name______________________________ Date ____________

What to Ask	What to Look For	Results
Where is the cover?	Student points to the cover.	☐ Yes ☐ No
Where is the title?	Student points to the title on the cover.	☐ Yes ☐ No
Where is the author's name?	Student points to the author's name on the cover.	☐ Yes ☐ No
How should I open the book?	Student correctly demonstrates how to open the book.	☐ Yes ☐ No
Where is the first page?	Student points to the title page.	☐ Yes ☐ No
Where is the top of the page?	Student points to the title at the top of the page.	☐ Yes ☐ No
Where is the bottom of the page?	Student points to the author's name at the bottom of the page.	☐ Yes ☐ No
(Turn to pages 4–5.) Where are some words? Where is a picture?	Student points to any words on page 4. Student points to the photograph on page 5.	☐ Yes ☐ No
Where should I start reading?	Student points to the first word on page 4.	☐ Yes ☐ No
How should my finger move as I read?	Student moves finger left to right under the line of print.	☐ Yes ☐ No
Can you point to the words as I read this line?	Student correctly demonstrates one-to-one matching as you read.	☐ Yes ☐ No
How many words are in this line?	Student correctly identifies the number of words in the line.	☐ Yes ☐ No
Where is an uppercase letter on the page?	Student points to an uppercase letter at the beginning of any sentence.	☐ Yes ☐ No
Can you point to the first letter in a word?	Student points to the first letter in any word.	☐ Yes ☐ No
Can you point to the last letter in a word?	Student points to the last letter in any word.	☐ Yes ☐ No
(Point to a period on any page.) What is this punctuation mark? What does it mean?	Student says, "Period." Student says, "It tells you to stop because the sentence is done" or gives a similar explanation.	☐ Yes ☐ No
(Point to a question mark on any page.) What is this punctuation mark? What does it mean?	Student says, "Question mark." Student says, "Someone is asking something" or gives a similar explanation.	☐ Yes ☐ No
(Point to an exclamation point on any page.) What is this punctuation mark? What does it mean?	Student says, "Exclamation point." Student says, "It means you use an excited voice" or gives a similar explanation.	☐ Yes ☐ No
(Point to a comma on any page.) What is this punctuation mark? What does it mean?	Student says, "Comma." Student says, "It tells you to pause" or gives a similar explanation.	☐ Yes ☐ No

Sight Word Assessment

Name________________________________ Date________________

Title	Sight Words	Date	Comments
Animal Babies	I, play, with		
Animals on the Farm	see, some, we		
At Grandma's House	had, we		
At My School	a, is, mom		
At the Shore	at, look, the, we		
Big Pet, Little Pet	big, is, little, this		
Count Around the Room	has, he		
Count at the Baseball Field	have, we		
Count on Me	has, she		
Counting With Mom	and, I, mom, see		
Dad Likes New Clothes	a, dad, wants		
Finding Shapes With Dad	dad, said, see, the		
Finding Stripes	see, the, with		
Going Up and Down	go, the, they, up, down		
I Am Active	am, I		
I Go!	a, go, I, in		
I Like the Spring!	I, like, the		
I Like to Play Sports	I, like, play, to		
In Our Town	goes, mom, the, to		
In the Band	at, look, the		
In the Water	I, in, play, the		
Jobs Around Town	are, we		
Look and See	at, look, that		
Look at the Coins	a, here, is		
Look at the Shapes	can, see, the, you		
Look at the Sky	can, see, the, you		
Look at the Weather	can, I, see, the		

Sight Word Assessment

Name______________________________ Date_______________

Title	Sight Words	Date	Comments
My Family	is, me, my, this		
My Favorite Places	I, the, to, went		
My Home	at, look, my		
My Pet	likes, me, my		
My Town	here, is, my		
On My Desk	are, the, there		
Our Tag Sale	a, get, we		
Playtime at Home	play, they, with		
See the Birds	do, see, the, you		
Snack Time	had, some, they		
They Grow Plants	have, they, will		
Time to Eat!	at, eat, the		
We Go to School	go, the, to, we		
We Have Fruit	have, we		
We Like Birthdays	like, the, we		
We Like Vegetables	all, like, we		
What Goes Up?	goes, that, up		
What Has Stripes?	has, the		
What Is the Time?	is, it		
When I Grow Up	a, be, I, will		
With My Friends	a, all, to, we, went		

Bibliography

Allen, J. 1999. *Words, Words, Words.* Portland, ME: Stenhouse.

Beck, I. L., M. G. McKeown, & L. Kucan. 2002. *Bringing Words to Life: Robust Vocabulary Instruction.* New York: Guilford Press.

Blevins, W. 2002. *Building Fluency: Lessons and Strategies for Reading Success.* New York: Scholastic.

Buell, M. J., M. S. Burns, & A. Love. 2007. "Writing: Empowering literacy." *Young Children* 62, no. 1: 12–16.

Clay, Marie. 2005. *Literacy Lessons Designed for Individuals (Part One: Why? When? and How?).* Portsmouth, NH: Heinemann.

Clay, Marie. 2005. *Literacy Lessons Designed for Individuals (Part Two: Teaching Procedures).* Portsmouth, NH: Heinemann.

Clemens, J., E. Patterson, & M. Schaller. 2008. "A closer look at interactive writing." *The Reading Teacher* 61: 496–497.

Cole, A. 2006. "Scaffolding beginning readers: Micro and macro cues teachers use during student oral reading." *The Reading Teacher* 59: 450–459.

Diller, D. 2007. *Making the Most of Small Groups: Differentiation for All.* Portland, ME: Stenhouse.

Dowhower, S. L. 1989. "Repeated reading: Research into practice." *The Reading Teacher* 42: 502–507.

Fountas, I. C., & G. S. Pinnell. 2007. *The Continuum of Literacy Learning, Grades K–2: A Guide to Teaching.* Portsmouth, NH: Heinemann.

Fountas, I. C., & G. S. Pinnell. 2006. *Teaching for Comprehending and Fluency: Thinking, Talking, and Writing About Reading K–8.* Portsmouth, NH: Heinemann.

Gill, S. 2006. "Teaching rimes with shared reading." *The Reading Teacher* 60: 191–193.

Hasbrouck, J. E., C. Ihnot, & G. H. Rogers. 1999. "'Read naturally': A strategy to increase oral reading fluency." *Reading Research and Instruction* 39, no. 1: 27–18.

Horn, M., & M. E. Giocobbe. 2007. *Talking, Drawing, Writing.* Portland, ME: Stenhouse.

Juel, C. 1991. "Beginning reading." *Handbook of Reading Research*: 759–788. New York: Longman.

Kame'enui, E. J., D. W. Carnine, R. C. Dixon, D. C. Simmons, & M. D. Coyne. 2002. *Effective Teaching Strategies That Accommodate Diverse Learners.* 2nd ed. Upper Saddle River, NJ: Prentice Hall.

Kame'enui, E. J., D. C. Simmons, S. Baker, D. J. Chard, S. V. Dickson, B. Gunn, S. B. Smith, M. Sprick, & S. J. Lin. 1997. "Effective strategies for teaching beginning reading." *Effective Teaching Strategies That Accommodate Diverse Learners.* Columbus, OH: Merrill

Koskinen, P. S., & I. H. Blum. 1986. "Paired repeated reading: A classroom strategy for developing fluent reading." *The Reading Teacher* 40: 70–75.

Kuhn, M. R., L. M. Morrow, & P. J. Schwanenflugel. 2007. "The family fluency program." *The Reading Teacher* 60: 322–333.

Mayer, K. 2007. "Emerging knowledge about emergent writing." *Young Children* 62, no. 1: 34–40.

McGee, L. M., & J. A. Schickendanz. 2007. "Repeated interactive read-alouds in preschool and kindergarten." *The Reading Teacher* 60: 742–751.

McVicker, C. 2007. "Young readers respond: The importance of child participation in emerging literacy." *Young Children* 62, no. 3: 18–22.

National Reading Panel. 2000. "Teaching children to read: An evidence-based assessment of the scientific research literature on reading and its implications for reading instruction." Available at http://www.nichd.nih.gov/publications/nrp/smallbook.htm.

Peck, S. M., & A. Virkler. 2006. "Reading in the shadows: Extending literacy skills through shadow-puppet theater." *The Reading Teacher* 59: 786–795.

Prescott-Griffin, M. L., & N. L. Witherell. 2004. *Fluency in Focus: Comprehension Strategies for All Young Readers.* Portsmouth, NH: Heinemann.

Rasinski, T. V. 2003. *The Fluent Reader: Oral Reading Strategies for Building Word Recognition, Fluency, and Comprehension.* New York: Scholastic.

Rasinski, T. V. 2000. "Speed does matter in reading." *The Reading Teacher* 54: 146–151.

Rasinski, T., C. Blachowicz, & K. Lems. 2006. *Fluency Instruction: Research-Based Best Practices.* New York: Guilford Press.

Samuels, S. J. 1985. "Automaticity and repeated reading." *Foundations for a Literate America*: 215, 230. Lexington, MA: Lexington Books.

Trelease, J. 2006. *The Read-Aloud Handbook.* 6th ed. New York: Penguin Books.

Notes